I0839616

Hearts Beat with Band-aids

Written by Peter Lopez
Illustrated by Peter Lopez

For

Lord John Richard Carrington Lambert the 3rd, Katelyn McDowell,
David Kusher, Alex Bussey, Tyler Yosha, and Emily Reedy.

and

In loving memory of

Trey Lewin, Felix Lopez, Jacob Crespo, Juan Crespo,
and Katrina.

Table of Contents

Hearts Bleed   1

Time's a Band-aid   35

Hearts Beat with Band-aids.   86

To Whomever It Concerns.   108

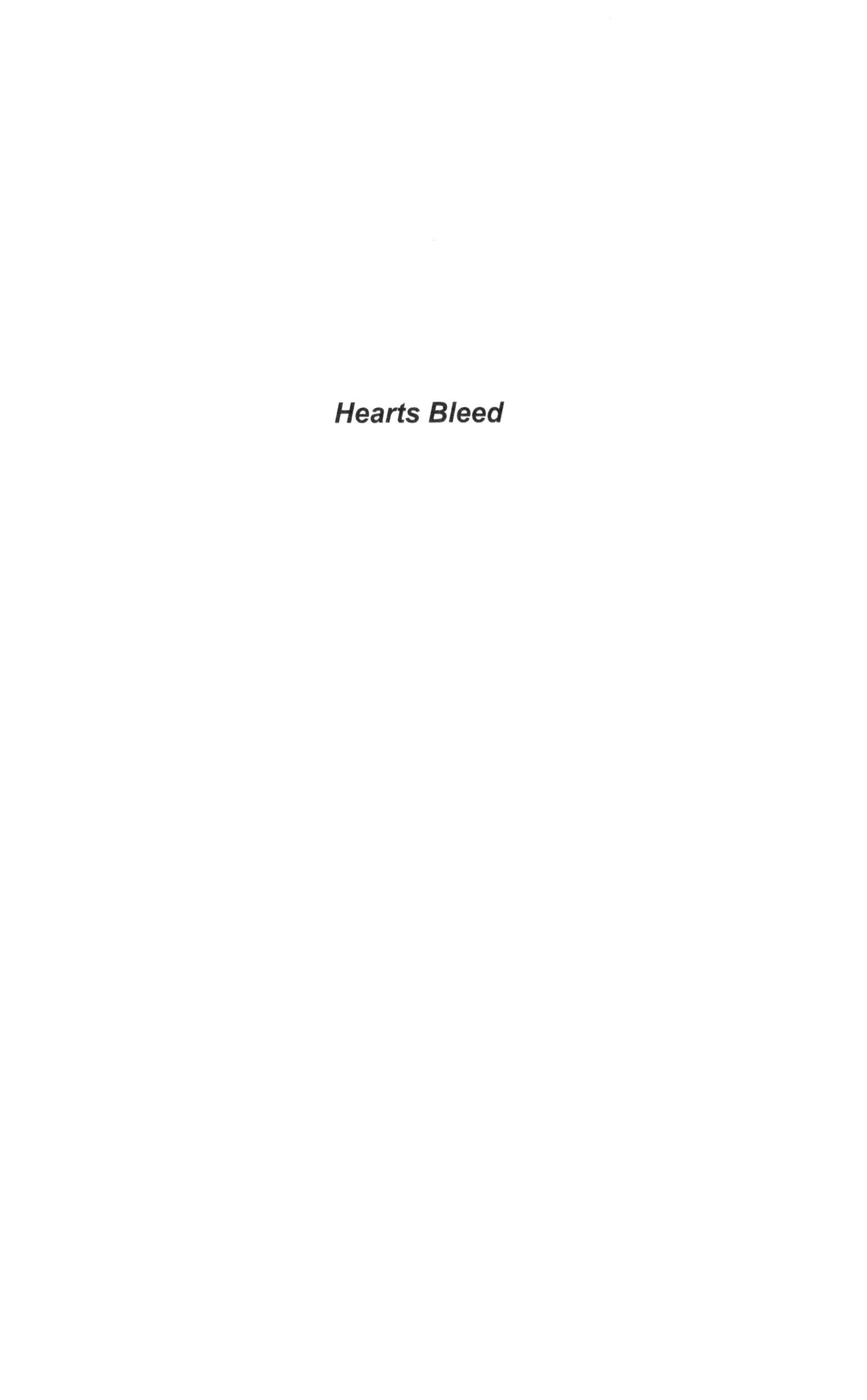

Hearts Bleed

Was it?

I'm scared to be okay.
I'm scared that once I inevitably let you go, it would mean I was wrong and that it wasn't love.

Love should be never ending. It
should be this magical fairytale
that's unbreakable.

But if after enough time, the love I
had for you is gone;
Was it ever even love?

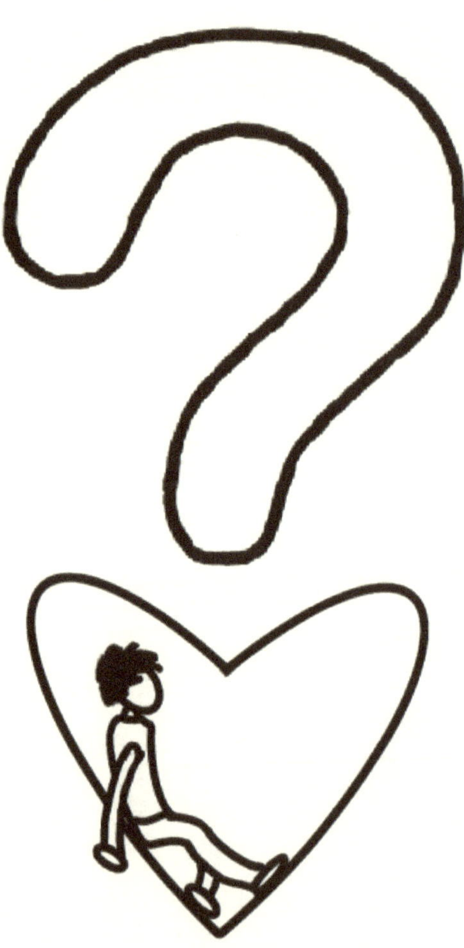

Peter Lopez

Lover boy

Being a lover boy is hard work.
You love everyone, love the idea of love, love seeing people in love: you just love, loving.
It's like getting on a rollercoaster that's being built as you ride. You don't know where it's going, you're in fear of crashing, but you love it. You always get on, you can't help it.

That's what it's like to be a lover boy. You fall in love with everything and everyone at least one time.

There's just one problem. One minor hiccup in what's imagined to be non-stop fun. A "what if"?

What if they don't feel the same? What if I'm irrational? What if they have someone already? What if they actually hate me? What if it's only a faked tolerance?

What if.
What if.
What if.

It leads to heartbreak.
And when a lover boy's heart breaks-
Then what?

Hearts Beat With Band-aids

I'm here again.

Waiting for you to see me,

Only for your eyes to walk past me.

You glance past my beating heart,

Passing up the warmth of my skin,

Leaving behind my being as a whole as if it was trash in a desert barren from not just man but any life itself.

You don't see me yet I'm here again and again.

I'm next to you like the sun rays that brighten your day,

Yet you'd see the wind across the seas faster than my own presence.

Why?

Why must you treat me as a ghost while having eyes from a non-believer?

Why can't you see I've been here?

I've been here, again, and again.

Ghost.

Go.

Watching you go was faster than written words could be read.
You left.

Not in a hurry.
Not a rush in the world.
But it was too fast for comfort.

Each step felt like melting ice cream.
Each drop I wanted to savor doing nothing but fall through my fingers.
And through my fingers it fell to the floor beyond my grasp.

Beyond what I could save.
Beyond what I could have.
You left and I watched you go.

Each step for you was maybe as normal as every other.
But each step you took,
To me was an eternity I wouldn't get to spend with you.

And in those steps,
I got to see all the things we wouldn't do.
I saw to see every moment we wouldn't share.
I had to see every memory we'd make stay a dream.
I got to see everything I didn't want to.

And I got to see it all,
As I watched you go.

One hundred.

I put our names in love calculators.
Those stupid websites that tell you a percent of how in love both names are.
And when we got low scores I'd get upset and reroll it.

I would reroll it until we got a one hundred.
I wanted us to have a one hundred.
I thought we deserved to have a one hundred.

It's embarrassing to say but it was like a ritual for me to do once a night.
A stupid little guilty pleasure that would make me blush that when I read a one hundred percent after try after try I would almost send you a picture as proof it was meant to be.

I wanted a one hundred percent,
Because I loved you one hundred percent.

Instagram.

I have you blocked on instagram, but I still see you in each swipe.

In every couple's post I still wish that it were us. I wish it was me reading the stupid comments of #need or me and who rather than being the one leaving them.

I have you blocked on instagram but it's not enough. I can't get rid of the memories we've made and can't stop myself from wishing we could've just made at least one more.

I open that damn app, and see something that I either wish was us, or something I'd send you and we'd laugh about.

I have you blocked on instagram, and I wonder if you see the same things I do.
I have you blocked on instagram, and I wonder if you wish you weren't.

I have you blocked on instagram, and I wish you weren't.

Hearts Beat With Band-aids

I can't hate you; yet at the same time I hate everything about you.

You treat me like the nails on your finger.

I scratch your every itch, open every can, I even remove the gunk from your teeth.
I do so much more than you think that you take for granted.

And like those same damned nails, you cut me out.

You made a home in my heart that I used to keep you warm in the coldest of days
and the harshest of storms.
In the midst of winter you made yourself welcome and like the fool I was I took care
of everything I needed to.

A fool who wanted to serve your every need.
A fool who did it with a smile.
And you matched my smile with a grin of unintended lies.

You wrapped my soul with a blanket colored with smiles that sing a siren's song.
You led my heart to the ocean with your song and it dived into the palms of your
hands without question.

And ever since that day,

I wanted your heart like birds need a sky.
Ever since that day,
I admired you like the stars in the galaxy.

And like most those stars in the galaxy,
You never knew I was there.

If you were Achilles,
I'd be your boots.
If you were drowning,
I'd be that first fresh breath of air.

I would be everything you'd need.

And everything you'd need, was something I wanted to be.

As the world turned,
I found myself learning things I couldn't bear.

You don't want me and now,
You no longer need me.

So all that's left for me is to say good-bye.

Good-Bye.

Handshake.

We have a handshake.
When I see you, we get excited and we do our handshake that we came up with
when we were studying late one night in a library.

It's so stupid; but it makes you laugh.
It's so stupid; but I love it.
It's ours.

It's all that will be ours.
Because at the end of that night you went home with him.

At the end of the day, you're still his.

You kept me up again last night.
You didn't snore, nor make a peep.
Not a sound to be heard,
Not a problem to be had.

Right?

God I wish.

I wish it were as easy as telling you to shut up.
I wish all it was, was just an easy solution in general.

Because you're not even in the room. You're not in the house at all.
I don't even know where you are. What I do know is that:
I just wish you you were here.

And that's the problem.

You're not here.
You're not in any chapter of my life and I continue to write you.

I write you, wishing I were writing us instead.

Write.

Hearts Beat With Band-aids

I don't believe in wishes.

All the shooting stars are just planes.
All the clocks skip 11:11.
All the candles on my birthday cake are LED.
All the hairs from my eyelashes weren't mine.
All the coins I threw into the fountains got picked up.
All the ladybugs are dead.
All the dandelion seeds blew in the wrong direction.
All the first stars came in second place.

Because if any of those were real.

Your hand would still be in mine.
Your phone would still have my number.
Your voice would be in my ears instead of my head.

If any of those worked.
Any at all.
You'd be here.

Wishes.

Ache.

Poets write poems, like clouds drop rain.
A lover boy will foolishly love, like a heart will have beats.

But not every poet's poem gets shared.
But not every cloud's raindrop kisses a plant.
But not every lover boy's love gets shared.

And ever since you left, my heart's never beat; it's only ache.

Hearts Beat With Band-aids

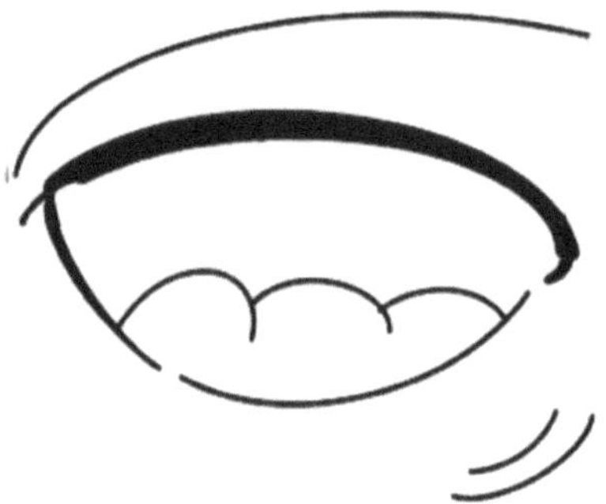

My eyes are like clouds, and you made it rain.

Clouds.

July.

It's raining.

Not a slimmer of sunlight is able to leak through the clouds and the puddles are high enough to kiss our ankles.

It was supposed to be a sunny day in the midst of our July.

We were supposed to go out on a picnic and I was supposed to feed you strawberries cause they're your favorite.

We were supposed to hold hands while we walked along the park.

But it doesn't matter.

Because you're at his place right now.
And I'm still foolishly imagining us.
And it's still raining in the midst of July.

Person.

You're in someone else's words.
It's gotten to the point where people will talk about you without them knowing they are.

People will ask how I've been and I'll reflect on if we've had any interaction.
It's not fair how my days have become dependent on if we've talked even just once.

You're just that person to me now.
That person who hijacks my train of thought anytime I get asked about a special someone.
You're the person that comes to mind in anything romance.
You're the person whom I want so badly to call mine.

But I can't.

Because you're someone else's person.

Hearts Beat With Band-aids

It's not my job to make sure you're okay.
It's not my job to make sure that you're loved.
It's not my job to make sure you're being treated right.
It's not my job to make sure that you're not stressed.

It's not my place to give you everything you've ever wanted.
It's not my place to give you the love you might need.
It's not my place to treat you the way I dream of.
It's not my place to share your stress.

It's not my job.
It's not my place.
It's not my anything.

I only want it to be.
But you picked someone else.

Not My Anything.

Friend.

You treat me like a friend and that's what hurts the most.

A Lot Of Things.

I want to carve our initials into the side of a tree.
I want to put a heart around them too.
I want to take a nap with you on a picnic date under that tree.
I want to give you a piggyback ride back because you hurt your foot.

I wanted a lot of things.
You wanted them too.

I'm writing another poem about doing it with you.
You're doing it with someone else.

Everything's got a label.

Live near the countryside,
And suddenly you're a country man.
Live near the city,
And then you're a city boy.
Looking for any thrills,
And you're an adrenaline junky.
Looking for hope in life,
And you're a lost soul.

If you have ambition,
You're a dreamer.
If you dream of her,
You're just another fool.

Label.

Special.

I thought I was special.

You didn't treat me in any fancy way.
You acted normally.
You acted like a friend should.
You did everything correctly.

I just wanted it to be different for me.
I wanted to be something else with a different meaning.
I know you don't see anything between us like that but I can't help it.

It hurts to try to read in between lines that aren't there for me.
It hurts to know the words are spoken to someone else.
It hurts to know they're there, just not for me.
It's not your fault, you didn't mean to do anything.
Just like I didn't mean to fall in love.

Peter Lopez

Time Spent.

When I was with you, not a second was wasted.
When I was with you, every minute was cherished.

When I was with you, the clocks ran faster.
When I was with you, time was ever more valuable and felt much more rare.

When I was with you, I was happy.

Now I spend my time remembering when I was with you.
Now I spend my time wishing for more of it when I was with you.
Now I spend my time missing when I was with you.

Now I like my time spent thinking about when it was time you wanted to buy.

You're my favorite bad memory.

Each time we've talked flows through my mind like a cozy warm river rapidly slamming into each corner of my heart.

I love to think about them all.

How each touch we've shared, it's like needles to my veins.
How each word that's left your tongue to grace my ears is like a paper cut from a love letter.

How can something I love; be so damaging?
How can something so damaging, feel so worth it?

Bad Memory.

Bridge.

When I met you I thought I was the luckiest person in the world.
Someone so genuine and kind.
But how could someone so *genuine,* make the bridge that connected us out of glass and feathers?
How can someone so *kind* expect me to cross a bridge like that?
How could you look me in the eyes with a match in one hand and smile at me?

Then again, how could I fall for it so easily?

Hearts Beat With Band-aids

The drops slow danced in my eyes.
They played the slowest song they could find and moved in harmony.
They danced and danced on my pupil of a dance floor.
They soon broke out of the chamber in my eyes, and
They danced on my cheek.

With only a legacy of red eyes and wet lines where they once danced to remember them, more tears began to dance to replace them as they stumbled down my face to leave.

Soon all I could see was the dancing of my tears.
The dancing that only grew more rampant and intense with each step you took.
The dancing that moved to the tunes of your words *"good-bye."*
The dancing that blocked the innocents of my eyes to the back of your head.
The dancing that made your increasingly smaller figure a blur.

A blur that danced to the beat of your steps.

Dance.

Peter Lopez

Dusty.

Our memories are getting dusty.
The places we loved grow old and only have the vines to keep it company.
The ghost of what we used to be haunts it, but only in our minds, or at least it does to me.

I drive past what was our spot and see us talking.
I see us laughing and smiling, unaware that those moments are limited.
I live my life walking backwards from time to time to look back at what we had. To see what was oh so scarce but still in demand.

But like the unseen side of the moon, and as mysterious as the stars we can't see you move forward like nothing even happened.
And I hate that. I hate that you don't care. Or I hate that you act like you don't care.
I'm left in shambles wishing that we were next to those growing vines, keeping those ghosts away and that instead of looking back we were walking forward.

But instead the memories will get dusty and dusty.

You and I.

In my eyes we were perfect.
The "*have it all*" couple.
The people that get pointed at by jealous singles.
The *perfect* pair.

To me;
We were like pancakes and syrup,
We were like butter and bread,
We were like shampoo and conditioner,
We were like stairs and railing.
We were like birds in the binoculars of bird watchers.
To me, we were everything.

But maybe I was wrong.
I must be wrong, because if I was right then we would still be we but instead it's you and I.

You and I didn't work out.
You and I went our separate ways.
You and I are just another story for someone to tell why love isn't real.
You and I are like a show that got canceled.

A show I loved.

To you, I wonder what you saw.
To you maybe we were sauce between fingers.
To you maybe we were nails on chalkboards.
To you maybe we were a first floor and second floor only bound by sheer dumb luck named stairs.
To you maybe we were a yellow sock and green sock in brown shoes with pink pants,

To you it was a mistake.
To me it was the best mistake you've ever made.
And maybe that's why, now it's only *you and I.*

Peter Lopez

Comfort Food.

I eat your comfort foods when I miss you.

We shared everything when we shared time.
We shared stories and dreams like cars share roads.
We know each other like kids know innocence.
We know each other like age knows time.

We are the best thing that's happened to me, dare I say us.

I don't want this *"we"* to become *"what used to be"*.

I love us more than red wet eyes love a rainy day to hide away.
I love us more than skin holding jackets in the midst of winter.
I love us more than music in ears.
I love us because it takes you to make it us.

And I think it's safe to say that we love our relationship as much as you love his lips
on yours.

We love it so much that you moved away and I helped you with a smile.
We love it so much that we talk just as much as we did before knowing the distance
between us is growing.

We love us to death.

It's why it kills me to know that the lips I share conversations with are kissed by a
pair that aren't mine.
It kills me to know I'm missing out on something I almost could've had.

I don't mind because we love us to death and I know we do because it's killing me.

I don't mind.
I swear I don't mind.

I have *our* comfort food to keep me company.

Hearts Beat With Band-aids

I can't forget you.

Like the second the lights strike your face from a flashing camera, and the inks steal that moment to give to a polaroid to be held for all eternity.

Like a word's legacy in a dictionary to be shared upon passing generations to avoid being forgotten.

Like the way grass will always be drawn green and the way our sun will forever shine yellow.

You will forever be a sensation my hand misses.
You will forever be a taste my lips wonder of.
You will forever be a song my ears loved hearing.
You will forever be a sight my eyes drew paintings of in my mind.
You will forever be a good memory.

And a memory is all you'll ever be.
Because you are forever gone.

Forever.

Peter Lopez

Stain On Paper.

I pour the emotions my heart leaks onto pens and stain pages with it.
I write the things my tongue could never say with it.

I write and I write,
I write and I write.
I write until the words can only be distinguished from the racing of my heart
because my mind can't process the weight of each sentence anymore.

I write for the light to glow upon my art to let my ink dry.
I write for the ink to dry in a way that is beautiful.

It will never dry, it will always be a mess, and I will never be satisfied.
No matter how many pages with ink shine under the sun,

Until it shines under the light from the glow of her eyes;

it's a pointless stain on paper.

If I had to describe us,

I'd say we're like the sun and moon.
I'd say we're like stars and eyes.
I'd say we're like heads and toes.
I'd say we're like roads and planes.

We just couldn't be further apart if we tried.

Describe.

Jokers

How silly must a lover boy be, thinking he could win a queen of hearts with a hand of jokers.

Mouth.

Your new boyfriend chews with his mouth open.

You moved on. When we were done you shopped around for a new boy, and I was left with less than nothing.

I stalked your instagram and you acted as if I never happened. The photos that should've been us were stolen with him instead.

I looked at your follow button and it was colder than the shoulder you gave me when you walked past me.

Your new boyfriend chews with his mouth open.

I saw his tag in your post and couldn't help but see my replacement.

What did he have that I didn't?
What part of him was able to keep you?
What part of me drove you to him?

I looked and saw everything wrong.
You and him would never work.
He's clean as can be, but when he talked it was filth.
Last night's lies were wedged in his teeth, and the stink of fake love emitted with his words.

Your new boyfriend chews with his mouth open and it's filthy.

He's perfect for you.

Time's a Band-aid

I can't sleep.

I can't sleep anymore.
I've moved on but the dream world still escapes me and I'm left with open eyes.

I've gotten used to the spirit of your voice echoing through my empty room.
I've gotten used to the cold room resting on my face as my blankets try to hold me the same way you did.
I've gotten used to holding my own hand at night and pretending the pillows are hugging me tight.
I've gotten used to wishing you were here, and sleeping in the comfort of my wishes.

Now I don't and I can't sleep once more.

The silence of my room is damning and while I don't miss you, I miss the uncomfort of missing you.
The room's a furnace and my blankets aren't competing to hold me anymore, I hate it.
The hand I used to hold myself is okay by itself now, and the pillows don't have to hug me.
The wishing you were here stopped and now the only comfort I wish for is wishing I weren't in need of wishing.

I can't sleep and I don't know who's fault it is.
I want someone to blame for this but I can't curse you and I don't want to curse myself.

Instead, I'll curse the days I slept for making me hate the days I couldn't.

Pages.

I have lists upon lists filled with words, and sentences of everything I want to say, and so much more.

I look at you, and everything makes sense. Just for a little while everything falls upon my pages perfectly.

The words I write have meaning.

But what about after?

You're long gone but the words I wrote are still there.

The only difference between them and now, is that the pages I used are wet with tears, and I can't look at them the same.

Now I'm left with pages filled with words that used to mean something to me.

Pages that used to carry a weight I was afraid to share; but pages you loved to read.

Now they're just pages with memories.

Forgiven.

I hate that you're not with me.

You're with him, God knows where, creating another memory that you're gonna tell me about.

You're gonna text, and call me and tell me every detail as if I'm not already imagining each and every scenario.

You'll look at me with that smile and tell me every perfect moment, and I'll look at you with mine as I nod and pretend it doesn't drive me mad.

I can't hate you for it, because that's impossible for me.

Hating you would make me feel worse.

Besides, I've already forgiven you.

Peter Lopez

Heart.

Memories are made to be forgotten.
Sights are seen to become memories.

The memories we make serve no purpose to anyone but us, but when we forget what's the point?
Everything we all see will have no effect once we forget.

You were smarter.

I might forget everything I've seen, I might even forget what it was like to be with you at sometime.

But my heart will forever beat the same way.

So instead of implanting yourself upon my memories and infatuating me.

You stole my heart and cut it with the tongue you spoke with.

Now when it beats, it beats with the scars you left.

Hearts Beat With Band-aids

You never forget your first.

We didn't do a lot, but to me it was enough.
Enough for it to drive me mad when you left faster than you came.

I still remember the times we FaceTimed, the times we stayed up till one AM texting.
Those nights where I'd get your text and giggle to myself and wonder if you were giggling too.

Were you giggling?
Do you remember those nights?
Do you also look back and smile?
Do you also miss it?

You replaced my opinion of you with a foul stench.
When you left me, you left me in a state of madness.
Life was more than uncertain and in a time where I needed company you accompanied me with space.

My text and calls were answered with automated messages and the foolish hope *"she's just busy. She'll get back to me later."*

Days passed and it was only me in our messages.

I clinged to those memories.

The memories I oh so desperately adored, and was addicted to remembering were quickly replaced with how I held my phone like it was your hand: How I buried my body into the couch cushions pretending they were your hugs.

Do you remember getting those texts?
Do you look back and remember swiping away to each and every plea?
Do you look back and smile?
Do you regret it?

Do you even remember my name?

Was I just like another fish in an aquarium for you to enjoy for a few minutes and forget about the next day?

I should be able to say I hate you.
I should be able to call you terrible.
I should be able to look back at everything and not care that you're gone.

But you were my first.
And you never forget those.

Just like I'll never forget those times we talked till the morning.
How we met up in those classes with dark circles in our eyes and we smiled at each other.
How we even wore matching Halloween costumes together.
How you sounded when you accidentally flashed me, and I pretended I wasn't paying attention to avoid you being self conscious.
How we flirted left and right and we cling to each other.
How I blushed uncontrollably when someone said we'd be good together cause we kept us a secret.

I'll never forget how you taught me to forgive.
Or how you taught me to be thankful.

Because thank you.

I love each of those memories.

First.

Brownie.

You are a terrible cook.
You made me a brownie and I hated it.

It was mushy and I forced every bite down. With each bite I'd strategize with pieces that you burnt to give it a texture I didn't mind.

Eating it was a chore, but when you looked at me and asked how it was.

I looked at you and told you I loved it.

I didn't lie.

I loved that you did something like that for me.
I loved that I was someone worth that time and effort.
I loved that I got to suffer ever so slightly because I was someone you cared about.

I loved that brownie, and I love that memory

Everything.

There are parts of you in everything.

I hear you in songs where your name isn't even spoken.

I look for your smile in a group that's laughing,

I even check my passenger seat when I break a little too hard to see if you're okay.

I even stare at the empty canvas of a chair, across from me and laugh to myself,

wondering what else you'd say if you were with me now in that same chair.

Each stranger I hold the door for, a part hopes you're hiding behind them waiting to say hello.

You're even in the stories I tell, because a part of me wishes that I got to share that memory with you.

Hearts Beat With Band-aids

I like my coffee sweet with milk.

I don't like my coffee black. I don't mind it but provided the option i'll take my coffee with sugar.
Days walk past my eyes and time denies my request of more. I wake up and take my coffee sweeter with milk.

You woke me up and I tried a new tea that was one of your favorites. Your *go-to* drink at this cozy little shop. I trusted your input and got the same.
I took a sip and hated it.

I drank my tea with a smile and you asked how it was.
I don't remember what I said, but I remember laughing. We told stupid stories and I learned more about you.

I don't like my tea fancy and overly flavored. I don't even buy the bags. I buy the gallons with the premade stuff because I could care less about the process and learn more. But the weird somewhat gross but not intolerable flavor is nice.

I like my tea sweet and with you.

Coffee n' Tea

Lucky

I fell in love with you.

You shared kindness like the wind gives a breeze. You shared memories that nobody else knew and sides I never thought I'd be lucky to know. How fortunate me, would ever get to share experiences with someone like you.

Experiences not even out of the ordinary, yet extraordinary.

Extraordinary because all because little ol me,

 fell in love with you.

I looked in your eyes and I haven't seen colors the same.

Since then, I can't look at the world and can't see it the same way I did before. Everything is just that much more lovely because it reminded me of you.

From the things you hate, the things you love, to wondering what you would say about anything. I'd get cut off in traffic and start smiling to myself like some idiot because I know you'd be so upset..

You'd rant to me and I'd do nothing but smile, because I'm the lucky guy who you picked to rant to.

I'm the lucky guy who got to fall in love.

Poet.

Poems like you were the reason why I didn't mind being a poet.

Miss me.

I don't want to write poems nonstop.
I don't want to resort to poetry each time I think of you.
I don't want to have a feeling and get these urges to write it in a way that's beautiful all the time.

I just want you.

I want you to see it in my eyes and the hesitation to tell you everything I think, all of the time.
I want you to look at my lips and suffer as you wonder what could've been.
I want you to have the urge to know what I'm thinking and feeling all of the time all of the day.

I want you to want me.

Or at the very least;
I want you to miss me back.

Hearts Beat With Band-aids

I'm so much happier now.

I love you and I'll always have that love for you; it just doesn't hurt to say it now.

I love you and it doesn't hurt to feel it anymore.
I love you and it doesn't weigh on my heart anymore.
I love you and there's no longer a tax on my time to sleep.
I love you and there's no longer a knot in my stomach tied to my throat to feel it.

I love you, and for once I don't mind.
I love you, and for once I'm glad I fell in love.
I love you, and for once I'm happy to say it.
I love you, and for once I don't feel the need to write about it.

Happier.

Moved on.

Time passed and looking in your eyes doesn't have the rope it used to bound my throat to my heart with. Time passed and as it walked on by it grabbed my hand and we talked about everything.

As I talked with time I told him all the things I told paper with ink, I told him I was scared to keep walking with him.
That I was scared to walk with him and only him.

He didn't care. He knew I didn't have a choice, and while I knew it I pretended I did.
And each chance I had I'd close my eyes for just long enough to think of you.

It didn't last long.

As we walked, he woke me up from the last time I'd think of you, the last time I'd dream of you.

Like the rain steals the dryness of a floor,
Like the thunder's cry takes the silence,
Like the lightning fools the world into thinking it's day for less than a second;

I forgot about you.
I moved on.

Lesson.

Feeling upset and hurt got tiring.
I kept writing poems about everything and had articles for it all.
I hated that it was all I could write about but at the time it was all I could feel, it was all
that I knew.
It was all that you taught me.

Whether you meant to or naught you taught me what heartbreak felt like.
You taught me what it was like to write poems in pain,
You taught me what poems about heartbreak looked like
You taught me sad songs and looking out at the rain wishing we were dancing in it.

Then I learned what moving on felt like,
Yet, that was the hardest lesson.

Not Anymore.

I wonder if you'd take me back.

I'm not the same boy you dated.
I'm not the same boy you left behind.
I'm not the same boy who watched you leave.
I'm not the same boy at all.

I wonder if we talked, if you'd feel bad for anything.
I wonder if we talked, if you'd wish you would've stuck around.
I wonder if we talked, if you'd ask to stick around.
I wonder if we talked, if I'd be willing to let you.

There's a famous saying:

Fool me once, shame on you.

I'm still a fool.

But I'm not the same boy.
Because I'm not a fool for you.

Not anymore.

Talking to you was the best part of my day.

Now I have to settle for remembering the conversations we had.

It's funny how time changes people, even the memories by giving things.

Things like the sting of regret,
The kiss of love,
Or the mercy of forgetting.

Regardless of what becomes of the conversations we had.
I'm glad I had them.

And I'm glad I had them with you.

Conversations We Had

I Love Them.

It took a while for me to write again.

You never knew it but you were the first person to get a poem.
You never knew it but you were the first person to know I loved poetry.
You never knew it but I wanted to write so many more poems for you.
You never knew it but you ruined it for me for so long after you left.

Writing anything would make me remember the worst of our relationship.
It would make me remember how open I was with you, just for you to pack up and
leave in the long run.

But I don't have to show these pages to anyone anymore.
I don't have to do anything with these.

I learned that these words are enough for me.
I learned that the words I've written are only for me to judge.
I learned that sharing the words I print doesn't make them anyless mine.
I learned that they aren't valued any less because the eyes of another see them in
different lighting.

These lines of ink I've left behind are mine.
These poems I've created, regardless of what they're about, are mine.

And I love them.

I don't like to cuss in my poems.
I see these words as delicate to the touch.
Each piece of ink on these pages is a kiss from my tongue.
And curse words are exactly what they sound like.
A curse placed upon the kiss I sculpt on each page with ink and a heavy heart.
So with a heavy heart and no lies to tell,
I mean it when I say you fucked me up.

Curse.

So Can I.

I think about you more than a car's headlights have seen red lights.
I think about you more than syrup raining on pancakes.
I think about you more than the eyes of a man seeing the palms of his hand.
I think about you more than the tongue of a human tastes in a day.

I think about you so much it's scary to think of a time I won't anymore.

But if you could do it, so can I.

One more time

I did it again,

I made myself fall in love with you just one more time.

I keep telling myself, I'll move on.

I tell myself I'll find someone new and perfect for me.

This is the last time I'll think of you with eyes that see just how much I'm missing out on.

That no matter how much it sucks, I won't come back to you.

I'll let myself love someone else just as much as I almost got to love you.

But I don't,

I forget about you and just one second after it, I'll miss you and go right back to square one.

I fall in love with you,

Just one more time.

Hearts Beat With Band-aids

Holding conversations.

Noise doesn't work for me anymore.
I tried to drown out the whispers of your ghost with conversations made between my friends and them talking to wherever the party leads them.

Music is never listen to on my own to drown myself from feelings I'm too scared to write about.

But it's not working anymore.

The music isn't loud enough and I don't even want to be here

I never did.

I thought trying something new would make me feel something new but I guess it doesn't work when that something was never you from the start.

I can be social.
I don't mind conversations with strangers but I'd rather hold them with people I know.

When you hold them with someone you know they have meaning.

When you hold someone you know it has meaning.

Talking with you had meaning and holding you gave those conversations more meaning.

But I can't hold onto this music anymore.
I can't take this noise anymore.

Not when it's pointless.
No author ever wrote a word worth a book with a pencil that had no tip.

Nothing ever good will come from parties I don't wanna be at.

That's why I'm in a corner writing this.

I know the noise isn't for me.

I know the parties aren't for me and I refuse to let myself hold conversations with someone that won't care the next day.

That's why I prefer holding a pen I love,
And holding conversations with a paper.

Because the noise is silent.

Imagine you're trying to catch a ball of yarn by its tail.
It's falling through your hands and you're frantically pulling it to you.

Through each frantic pull and heartbreaking tug to pull this yarn to you it's uncoils and uncoils.

Uncoils and uncoils.

Unraveling until it's nothing.

Then it's a mess on the floor and a massacre in your hands.

It didn't matter what I did.

The yarn's still gone and would've been away from me either way.

But I was scared and pulled.

Pulled myself into a mess I never needed.

Yarn.

Priceless.

There once was a love that was mutual between us,
Regardless of how long it lasted it was there.
There was a time we valued each other the same,
Regardless of what that value is now.

Now there's nothing but time to love myself,
Regardless of how you priced it for yourself;

I see it as priceless.

Lips.

The burning sensation traveled across each crevice engraved on my lips.
With each passing second I could feel the world getting hotter and my head getting lighter.

It hurts to look back on, but I loved each painstaking minute of it.
I'm addicted to the moments your lips are mine that ever so rarely come my way, and slither away even faster.

With eyes that blend into the stars, almost distracting me from the secrets you hide within.

A serpent's soul, and your scaled personality.
I know that each time we kiss it's nothing but venom, but it kills me more when I'm without them.

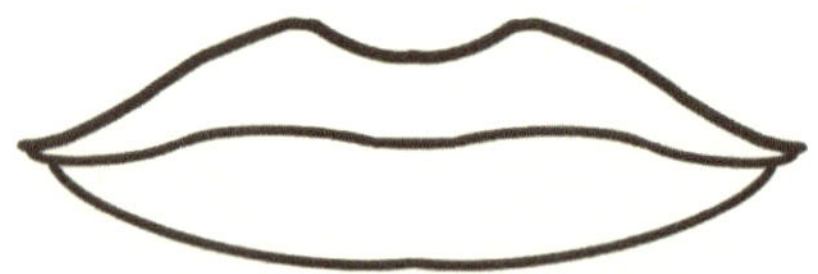

Peter Lopez

Call Me.

I want you to call me.

We text, and it's not that I hate that.
I'm addicted to reading the bubbles being typed on your side.

I just want an excuse to hear your voice one more time.
I just wonder who you call when you swipe past my name.

I just want you to call me.

Writing Us.

You'll forget my words.
It's only a matter of time.
Paper will remember ink till it's no longer paper.

Maybe that's why I love writing you.
Maybe that's why I love writing us.

Coaches Don't Play.

Coaches don't play.
It's a famous expression, and one that many friend groups apply to someone.

I'm the someone with that title.
I give advice, it's what I'm known for.
It's a scary thought because maybe I'm a coach.
What if, I'm a player on the bench.

How do you know for sure?
How does anyone know?

And if I'm benched;
Why?

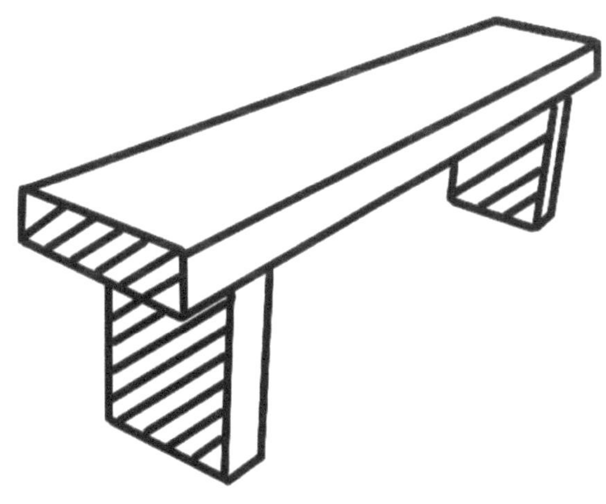

Hearts Beat With Band-aids

I might have ruined us.
I might have prevented what could've been.
I might have messed up something that would've been great.
I might have been the reason we aren't together.

But at least for a moment,
A moment or two.

There was an *us* in general.
And for that I'm so thankful

Us.

Vain.

You're in every poem.
Even the ones that aren't about you.

When I write about you I know it's in vain.
When I don't write about you, I'll wish I were.
When I write about anything I'll think about sharing it with you.
When I don't write anything, I'll want to write something to share.

Everythings been about you.
Everythings been done while thinking about you.

I just hope that doesn't mean everything's been in vain.

Saw.

My friends knew it before I did.

They saw small changes in how I talked and carried myself.
I saw myself being more comfortable and desires for change.
They saw my music taste change.
I saw myself branching out and learning.
They saw me falling in love.
I saw myself making a friend.
They saw me get my heart broke.
I saw it get shattered.

I say I've moved on,
They see through my lies.

When will the day I speak of moving on not be seen as a lie?

Peter Lopez

Nightmares.

It's two in the morning and I woke up my friend for company.
I can't seem to fall asleep anymore.
Anytime I doze off, you always wake me up.

Your smile screams at me the second my eyes close.
Your voice wanders the hallways of each dream.
Your ghost haunts the corners of my brain.

And when you don't.
When you're finally gone;
I'll wish you weren't.

No matter the dream I'll think of you.
Because if you're not in my dreams,

I'll call them nightmares.

Imagine.

Poems come easy to me.
I write at the thought of you almost instantly.

I've written time and time again.
I've written more poems about you than I wish I did.
I've imagined your reactions to these words and writing as I write each poem out.

I've only imagined.
All I've done is imagine.

Imagine the planes in the sky were shooting stars.
Imagine the puddles in my yard counted as fountains.
Imagine the dreams I dreamt of us were real.
Imagine that in some timeline you saw me the same.
Imagine that you'd look forward to each of my poems as I wrote them.

So cheers to my imagination

To which I'll imagine once more, a world where you wanted a poem.

And again I'll write a poem that you never wanted.

Moments.

I don't think I'm a sad person.
I'm a happy person that just has sad moments.

Sad moments that are only sad, cause they'll never happen.

Moments of us that were replaced with me writing about wishing for them.

While you go about your days.

A Boy.

I loved it when you talked to me.
The times you initiated conversation, you picked me.
All your friends, all the boys chasing you, even your family.

Me.
You picked me first.
You talked to me about problems and it was a struggle to focus on what you said, and not that you were here with me.

Me.
You picked me first.
You talked to me about a boy you were interested in. A boy you were talking to romantically. A boy I told you to chase if you cared that much about.

You did.

I secretly hoped it was me you were talking about.
I knew it wasn't.

You picked me first.
And I let you go last.

I wonder what it's like.

You'd grab my hand and look me in the eyes.
You'd smile and go "I love you".

Maybe you'd tap my shoulder and say it.
Maybe you wouldn't even touch me, you'd call my name and say "I love you".

I wonder what it's like.

Would you kick your feet up and smile as you texted me?
Would you cram your pillow into your chest as you blush?

I wonder what it's like.
I wonder how you'd act.

I wonder.
I *wonder.*

I wonder so much how you'd tell me if you did.

How would you tell me, *I love you.*

Wonder.

Bitter.

I wish I didn't see art in any and everything.
As a poet I see the beauty in everything,
As a wordsmith I know how to word everything.

But as a hopeless romantic, I feel the *hurt* in most things.
And as a foolish lover boy I know the bittersweet end things can come too.

With eyes that see art, and
With eyes that have seen your soul.
With a tongue that's kiss your words, and
With a romantic's desire of your heart.

I see you in every piece of art.
I see you in all things tied with the word *beauty*.

But as a lover boy I know our end is sweetless and bitter.
But I can't help but be a fool.

You forget our conversations.
The things that are important to me.
Our plans.

I get it, you're busy. How could you not be?
Little ol' you is busy with him so of course your friends are gonna skip your mind.

We aren't as important.

It's fair and it makes sense and I won't hold it against you.

Just like how I won't hold it against you when you forget us.

When you forget me.

Busy.

Not Yet.

I've stopped writing about you.
You're not a threat to my pen anymore.
You're not a plague that spreads through my poems with ink.

You're almost a distant memory.
I thought it would hurt.
But when I woke up and thought of you, my heart kept beating.

When I woke up I still saw my room
When I woke up with the same warmth I went to sleep with.
When I woke up I didn't need you next to me.
When I woke up, I didn't need to write you.

I just choose to now.
Not because I'm scared to let go.
Not because I can't let go.

I just don't want to.
Not yet anyway.

Peter Lopez

I learned to wear sunscreen.

I learned because touching you was like hugging the sun.
And I got burned.

Sunscreen.

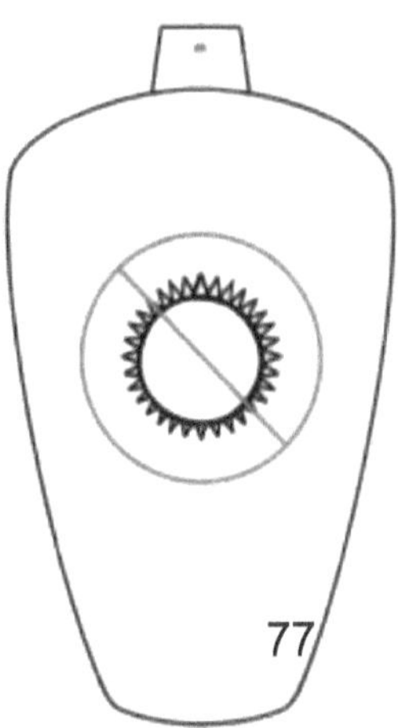

77

Would You?

If you could go back in time, would you still bump into me?
If you could go back in time, would you change your yes to a no?
If you could go back,

Would you?

I Remember.

I remember the times you'd sit next to me.
I remember the way you'd ever so slightly creep your hand into mine when you did.
I remember the way my heart would collide with my chest as if it were clawing to get out.

I remember it all.

Better or Worse.

Your name is tattooed on my soul.
Your actions have scar'd my heart.
For better or worse, I don't think I can forget you.
For better or worse, I don't think I'd ever want to.

Thoughts.

When I breathe, it's almost as if I want to speak.
My tongue shivers and my throat grabs the words in my head,
But it holds everything I want to scream hostage.

When I pick up a pen, my throat lets go,
And everything I'd scream fall to paper.
A paper you'll never read.
A paper with words you'll never know.

The thoughts I'll never share.
The thoughts that make me scared.

Pages and Ink.

Spotify calls me heartbroken.
My Spotify daylist consists of songs about being sad, and even has *heartbreak* in its title.

I don't feel heartbroken.
We didn't work out, but
It's not like I ever entirely lost you.
I still have you.
I'll always have you.

Not in flesh and blood,
But in pages and ink.

Only hope.

I hope you look for my arms in his hugs.
I hope you wish for my voice when he speaks.
I hope you wonder what I would say when he gives advice.
I hope you miss my jokes when you're laughing with him.

And I hate that I do.
But I hope it because then I'll be the better pick.
And maybe then I won't feel so guilty for hating him.

But for now,
I can only hope.

Story.

No matter where you are, I will still have been in your life.
At the end of the day, no matter how many of them have come in between our first and
last conversation.
We still had it.
We were something that existed.
No matter how many chapters you write in your life,
No matter how many characters appear on your side of the story:
I was in it.

I was in your life.
How will you tell your readers about me?
Would you?
Are your readers going to hate me?
Will they miss me, and beg for my return?

Will I return?

Do you want me too?

Midnight.

I wish I made your heart skip beats, like the way you pass over my text to open up his.
I wish I could kiss you so elegantly, like the way the sun strikes you at every perfect angle.
I wish for a lot of things that won't come true like some kid wanting to be a superhero.

I know I wish for simpler things like getting sleep.
I know that won't come true either because it's midnight and I'm up late writing this because I'm wishing for more of you.

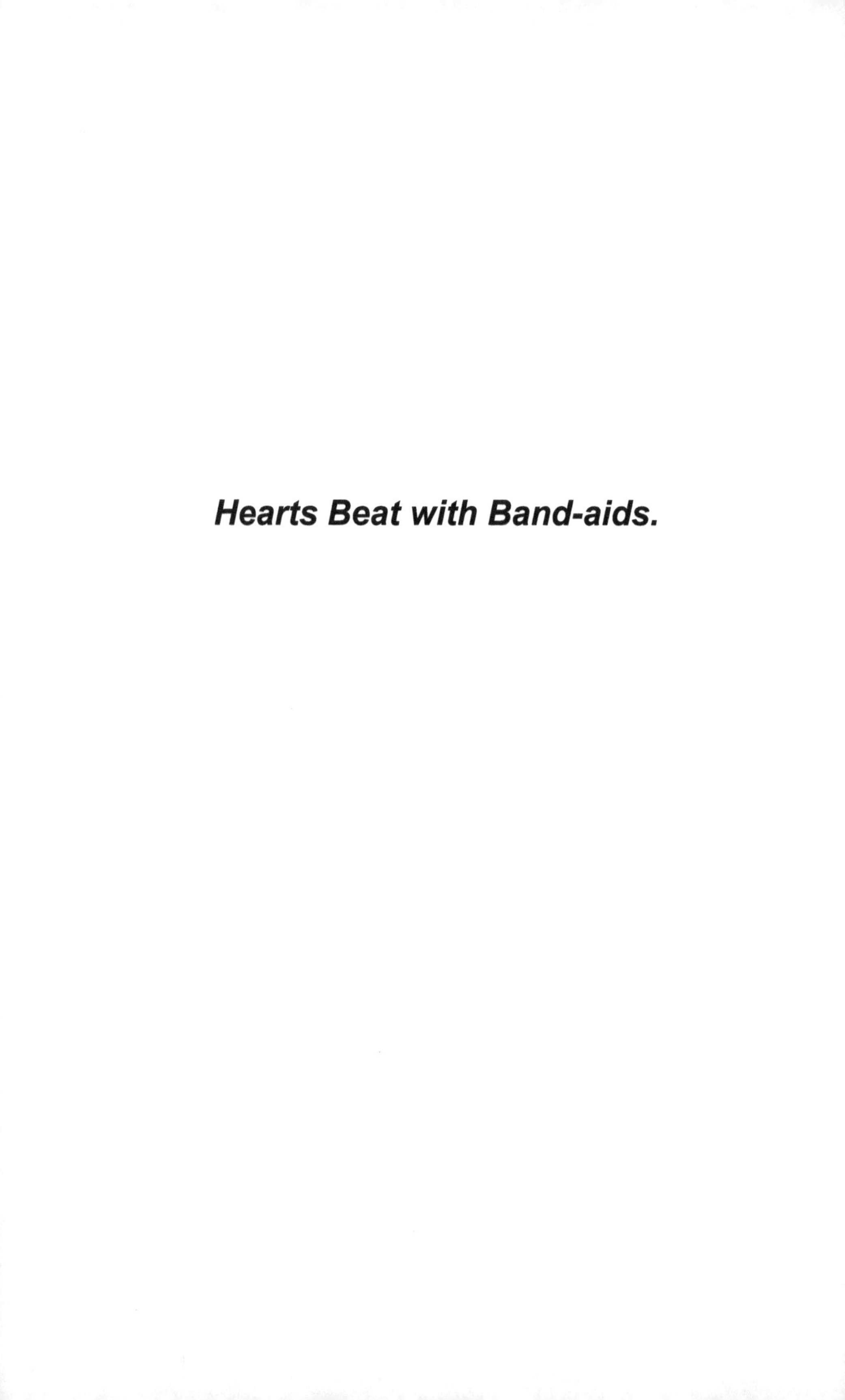

Hearts Beat with Band-aids.

I still think of you.

I wonder if you know that when you stare into my eyes, they remember you.

It's as simple as it can be really.

You capture my gaze like a new world in a baby's eyes, yet when you cross my mind, it's just another road to you. It's like it's not your first time doing this, and it isn't;

To me, it isn't.

Even when you're long gone the thought of you is still next to me like a ghost that haunts me.

You possess my mind like it's some puppet ready to be controlled at a whim's notice.

I don't even hate it.

You being semi there, just in thought makes me feel just a little bit less alone. It's weird I know, that you probably don't even remember much of me and here I am.

A prisoner to the thoughts of you.

It's weird, I know, but I wonder if you know that when you're done looking at me,

I still think of you.

Everything has an end.
From the songs we listen to,
From the days we cherish,
To the views we admire,
To the people we love.

Every good book has a last page.
That doesn't make the story unreadable.
It makes the story worth picking up.

Not because it's forever,
But because it took time to be created,
And therefore it exists and that alone is something to love and be thankful for.

From the unfinished pages,
The typos and misunderstandings,
The revisions, and the dialogue that was cut,
To the final artwork
To the final copy of each and every story.

It's not always an easy thing to do either.
Closing the book when you're done.
Saying goodbye to a loved one.
Walking away knowing it's the last time.
It hurts.

And it's okay for it to.
The hurting from a goodbye to anything,
Gives the value to a hello for everything.

End.

Honey.

Sometimes I don't know why I write.
Sometimes I don't know who I'm writing to.
Sometimes I write to a love I don't have, at least not yet.
Sometimes I want to write and it takes a longer time for the words to fall off my pen.

But sometimes bee's fly not knowing where to go.

They just have faith they'll find what they need to make honey.

A Poet First.

I don't know why I write poems.
For a while now, I'd think of you and get urges to write the things I wish I could say.
I don't mind that about myself.
I quite like it actually.

Being a lover boy and poet has its ups and downs.

But sometimes I wish I was a poet first.

What does a lover boy call it?

What is love?

There's not a guide book to what love is.

Trust me, I've looked it up and all there is are people telling you what would work but it's all just theories.

Google calls it a feeling of deep affection. Scientists call it a fluctuation of brain chemicals. Lovers call it beautiful and broken people call it torture.

What does a lover boy call it?

A lover boy who's done nothing but dream of his perfect love story. A lover boy who's seen bad endings and good endings in person. A lover boy who hopes he's not naive but still foolish enough to take a risk.

He calls it exciting.

So Much More.

Love doesn't end, not for me at least.
I'll forever care about you to an extent.

How could I not? You were my first and you taught me so much.

You made me hurt the most because
You made me feel the most.

I can't ever hate that so instead I'll love myself enough to let me love.
I'll love myself enough to love someone else just as much.
I'll love so much more than I thought possible.

His Favorite Thing.

I learned that when a lover boy's heart breaks,

It's only a matter of time.

It's only a matter of time before his heart heals.
It's only a matter of time before he's brave enough to take the band-aids off.
It's only a matter of time before he'll love again.

Because how could he not?

It's his favorite thing to do.

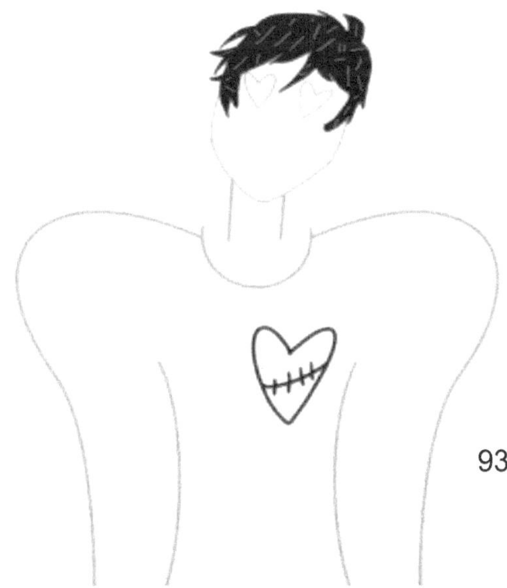

Lil lover boy

You changed so much in my life, and I'll never forgive you.

You knew I was a hopeless romantic, a *lil lover boy* even: I hate saying it, and it makes me feel corny but it's nothing I could ever deny.

So of course, being the *lil lover boy* I am, I could never see the word *pretty* the same after meeting you.

Before, *pretty* was just something that took my breath away. A sight to take photos, and share with friends and family. Something to talk about for a little and then forget about the next day.

I didn't forget.

The next day my breath was still gone, and my heart was still beating: I couldn't take photos because that's weird, so all I was left with was just a memory of the prettiest thing I'd seen, but was too embarrassed to share.

I couldn't tell a soul, not one but I needed to speak about this version of *pretty*: so I let you change how I write.

I wrote on and on about everything I could and everything I couldn't about you.

My hand learned how to talk about you with pages faster than I think anyone would ever like to admit. I wrote about everything I'd wanted to say to friends, and even more, you.

You're so damn pretty that I couldn't say it without being hypnotized.

You're so pretty that I don't mind being a lil lover boy.

Scream.

I want to scream it.
I want to scream it so loudly that nobody can hear it.
So I'll scream it with ink.

Each word I mark this page with, is one I'd scream till the star's shine is no more.
It has the feeling as if each line used to make a letter is its own nervous system.
My heart is in these poems.
That's why I write you so often.

Or at least I used to.

Now I whisper.

Catch.

When you fall down it hurts. Sometimes it even cuts.
When you fall, you get back up, even if you have to wipe a tear or two.
When you fall you still have somewhere to go.

When you fall in love, sometimes it hurts and will leave scars.
When you fall in love, time teaches you how to love again, even if you say you'll never do it again.

When you fall in love, someone will fall back.
You just have to be ready to catch them.

I lost my mind for you.

Almost everything I valued had a connection with you.
The connection I had as a whole was everything to me.

Then you left and took everything I had, including my mind.

Everything I thought about was you,

You were my favorite character in my own book.
You were someone I wished I had met sooner.
You were someone I hoped to be at the end of my story.

But like the cover of a book, and the summary in the back,
We couldn't be further apart.

I lost my mind for you.

I've only recently started making it whole.
I've only recently started enjoying the chapters that don't have your name.
I've only recently started to value the things that didn't make me think of you.

Now my mind is something I value because of it.
Now I wait to give it to someone else.

Mind.

A bruised heart can still beat.
And if a heart beats then it's capable of loving.
If it's capable of loving,

It's deserving of loving.

Bruised heart.

Enough.

I don't need help anymore.
I don't need to hear *I love you* from anyone to feel it.
I don't care about any external opinions, not anymore.
I don't think I do anyway.

For the longest time I needed to hear *I love you* to feel it.
I needed to feel loved in order for me to know it.

Not anymore.

When the sun leaves my eyes and the moon and stars come out to play,
If anyone else should follow the sun;
I will be okay.

I'll forever have poetry.
I'll forever have ink to write out whatever I feel.

To write whatever I need.

And that's enough for me.
I'm enough for me.
I'm enough.

Hearts Beat With Band-aids

The sunset is beautiful, isn't it.
The way the wave of colors painted the sky as the sun said farewell.

And with the sun's goodbye and the moons hello,
The river of colors splashed on the sky change from the fresh candy and gum drops to snow caps and sprinkles.

We looked at the change with nothing to say.
No thoughts to share; just time we traded for memories.

Memories all more memorable because they were made with you.

Sunset.

Matter.

It doesn't matter.
It doesn't matter if you've been broken before.
It doesn't matter how long you took to heal.
It doesn't matter if you're still healing.
It doesn't matter if the break in your heart is held together with tape's touch, glue's hug,
time's delicate kiss or love's grace.

It doesn't matter, and it never will.

Like the cracks on a sidewalk that leave its guest unaffected.
Like the space between clouds that remain unfilled.
Like the scars on bodies that only tell stories.
Like the holes on trees that add to its beauty.

It doesn't matter.

Each mark seen and unseen,
Noticed or missed,
Doesn't add or subtract to any value you have.

Scars on a beating heart doesn't matter,
So long as it's a heart you want to hold.

Once.

The hard part about writing poems is making sure I don't repeat myself.

I just hope you know that just because I wrote it once,
doesn't mean I thought of it any less.

Seven minutes.

After you die the brain plays your greatest memories for the next seven minutes.

For seven minutes you relive the best things in your life and I wanna make those minutes the best thing ever.

Seven minutes of laughing.
Seven minutes of clear skies in a full heart.
Seven minutes of eyes with no puff marks from tears.
Seven minutes of everything being worth it all.
Seven minutes of not wondering what's next because next wouldn't matter because I was here and here was all I cared about.

Just seven minutes.

Time feels so commonly out of my hands. no matter how much I look at clocks or wear a watch I'm always running after minutes that won't chase me back.

It's just seven minutes of a lifetime of memories.

If it really is only seven then I hope you're in at least one.

Hearts Beat With Band-aids

Tree.

I have separation anxiety.

It's nothing I haven't dealt with, it's a familiar game of cards where I get dealt and hand of jokers, and two's to deal.

It's an unfair game my heart makes me play from time to time,
I just never expected you to be the dealer.

Scratch that, I knew it the whole time.
I knew since the moments I shared stories like we share air like we share space on this planet that you'd be one of my favorites.

In a forest of trees held high you'd water saplings.
You didn't let the insects scare you.
You didn't care about getting a little dirty until you had seen what would become of a tree.

Tree's are all the same, just with different woods, branches and leaves.
Tree's are all the same, but some sing from up high while others whisper down below.

You wanted to see what tree I'd be and then make your own opinion.

People see trees with rough bark, no bark, all bark, rodents on branches.

I don't know what you saw but you watered that tree.

I respect that.
I love that.

And I'll miss the hands that picked up a watering can.
And I'll miss the voice that sang stupid tunes as the hands poured water.

But you'll be back in time.

Peter Lopez

It's just my separation anxiety

And even if you aren't, the cloud's will rain and sun will shine to give a tree all it needs.

So even if you don't, a tree will still grow.

And even if you don't, I'll remember the hand that poured water.

It taught me how to pour it myself.

Follow.

If you go your own way, I hope you let me follow you

Wherever your path leads, I hope there's room for two.

When you are offered extra things to share I hope I come to mind.

Just as you do for me.

When there's room on the sidewalk,

I want you there.

When I can't finish my food and want to give it away,

I would love to give it to you.

If I'm to run away,

I could only hope it would be us running together.

If I were to walk,

Would you follow me?

I dreamt that you kissed me.

I dreamt that you kissed me, and I woke up happy.

I sat up almost giggling to myself, with my toes curled and my heart racing.

I looked to my right, knowing you weren't there, knowing it was just some stupid dream, but hoping I was wrong.

Of course you weren't there, but I didn't mind…

I didn't mind because just for a moment, you were here.

I didn't mind because just for a moment you and I had kissed.

I didn't mind because just for a moment you were mine.

And to me, that was enough.

Dreamt.

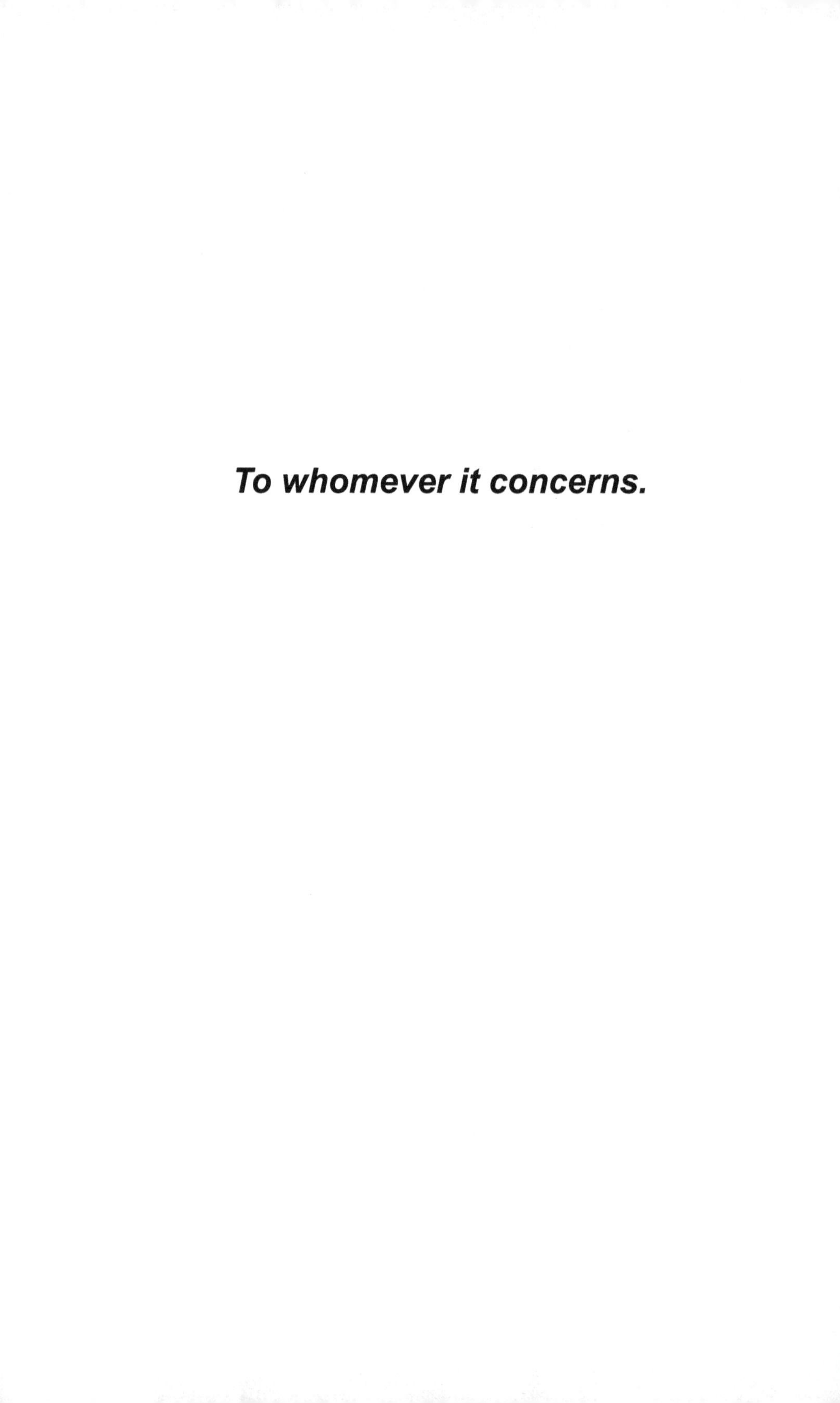

To whomever it concerns.

Intention.

Hi.

Hi, with the intention of talking to you.

Hi with the intention of spending my time wondering the best way of saying hello so I can say it just one more time another day.

Hi, with the intention of getting in a relationship, where every Halloween, we argue over what stupid characters we should match as.

Hi, with the intention of having late night talks where we both need sleep but want to hear each other's voice just a second longer.

Hi, with the intention of sharing each other's time while we talk about our dreams.

Hi, with the intention of spending minutes of my day being glad I'm with you, and hours wishing I were when I'm not.

Hi, with the intentions of falling in love.

Out your mind.

I look at you and smile.
I see you apparitions when you aren't there.
I frame every angle of you that you've ever shown me in every blank spot in my mind.

I've decorated my thoughts in all things you.
That might be crazy, which is kind of funny cause when they say *"you're out your mind"*

I couldn't disagree more.

I'm more in my mind than ever, and never want to leave.

You're there too.

Addicted.

I'm addicted to you.

I'm not scared to admit that I think about you, I'll even be the first to say that the best parts of my day include me wondering how you're doing.

I'm not scared at all.

You're a tattoo of a thought that I'd never be ashamed of.
Ink on my heart that I could never describe with paper.

I can't describe it.

The way your lips tease me as you speak.
The way you move your hands as you speak.
The way your hair slides down your shoulders and neck.
The way every feature you have works in perfect harmony for my eyes and heart.

Everything about you is just a song I could never bore off and every time we talk it's a personal concert.

I'm so addicted.

When I say.

I love you.

Love is a word that I don't say often in the way I'm saying it now.
Love is a scary thing to confess.
Love can be different between brothers, and friends, and friends you see as brothers.
It can be shown as differently as it can be felt so when I feel my tongue move to say I love you,

Everything I love about you is put into those three words, and they say that a picture can mean a thousand words:
Let me paint a thousand pictures I can only hope captures my I love you's.

When I say I love you;

I love the way the light drips around and makes you glow just a bit more,
I love the way you make colors brighter than they are,
I love the way the sounds I hear can't compare to any noise you speak,
I love the way you smile and how it draws lines across your face that I could only wish to write on.

I love when you call me and give me reasons to listen,
I love when you act like you so I can think "that's so you".
I love how each step you take gives the ground you walk on purpose,
I love how you squint your eyes as if seeing the things you're thinking helps you think.

I love you like the head of a flower leans on it's stem,
I love you like sails love wind,
I love you like a map loves a traveler,
I love you like a bird loves its wings.
I love you like I need to love you.

I love you for fun,
I love you for sad,
I love you for glad,
I love you for mad,
Because loving you is all I want to feel.

I need to love you the way a bee need's it stinger.
I need to love you the way butterflies were once caterpillars.
I need to love you the way glasses need eyes.
I need to love you the way memories were once decisions.
I need you.
I love needing you.

Peter Lopez

I need you like a theater needs an audience,
I need you like a book needs a writer,
I need you like a story needs telling,
I need you like the sun needs something to shine on,
I need you like a speaker needs something to say
I need you like a poet needs paper and ink.

I need you to know that when I say I love you,
I only say it because it's faster than writing this every time and so much more because
every time I write I think one thing more.

But if you need it, I'll draw the world in my I love you's.
But if you want more pictures captured, I'll treat my paper and ink like bait and a cage
and capture it all.
Should you want to hear it, I'll sing my words in tunes you'd love.
Should you need to feel it, I'll kiss you for good-night and good-bye and every hello and
my hi's.

So for now because now is all that we have,
I need you to know that when I say I love you,

I mean it.

Hearts Beat With Band-aids

Your flaw.

If your lips were knives,
I'd love the scars.
If your hands were flames,
I'd look forward to staying warm.
If your tears were acid,
I'd still wipe your face dry.

None of it would matter.

Because being without you would be worse than anything the cleverest of tricksters
could imagine.

Being with your every flaw is worth more than time spent with what absolute perfection
could give.

Voice.

Music doesn't sound *good* anymore.

Every love song is out of tune.
Every sad song is corny.
Every hype song is doing too much.
Every slow song is boring.

I guess sounds just aren't enough for me.
Maybe that's why I write.
Because when I read my words,
I imagine your voice.

Safe space.

You didn't leave.

Like most people,
I'll fascinate myself with something and it will be all to do for the next two or three
weeks.

I'll obsess over it.

Like starting a Minecraft world where all you do is play it.
Or keeping one song on loop until it gets old.
Swimming until you're tired and just can't anymore.

Mine was writing.
Spreading ink like it was news for the world to hear.
I'd convert the words I never would say to a face to a poem on paper.

Poems and poetry were my safe place.
I'd draw with words, poems that looked like you.
I'd create poems for you nonstop.
Before I knew it, the safe space for me was surrounded by your eyes.

I loved it.

The hobby of creating art in your name never stopped and the pictures of you that I've
written with ink and paper only grow and grow.

The two weeks became months, and God forbid I stop.

I don't want to stop.

You are my safe space now,
And I don't mind sharing it.

Peter Lopez

I like it when it rains.
The clouds cover up the sun, and it's nothing but gray as far as the eyes can see when you look up.
The rain drops clashing with my face as a crisp breeze reminds me I'm cold.
Everyone's running to get in doors, at least those who didn't get an umbrella.

Nobody's looking at anyone.
Nobody cares about anything except "*get inside*".
Nobody is focused on anything but the weather.

I like it when it rains.

There's nothing to think about.

No pretty sights to see.
No reason to be outside.
No reason to go anywhere but inside.
No reason to like the rain.

With nothing prettier to see I have all the more reason to look at you.
With nowhere else to go, I'm stuck under your umbrella that you wanted to share.
With an eagerness to get inside we're laughing as we splash in puddles and making a fool of ourselves.

We're acting like kids except we're both freezing and dripping because of the storm overtaking the umbrella clearly meant for one person.
We're sharing body heat to stay warm as harsh winds beat upon my soaked hoodie and your flooded jacket.
We're happy cause we're together in this terrible storm, making the most of an unfortunate situation.

There's no reason to like the rain,
No reason to like it unless I'm with you.

When it Rains.

Hearts Beat With Band-aids

I don't care.

I'll let everyone in the world drop my heart if it meant you'd get to hold it.

It doesn't matter how many band-aids I use,
It doesn't matter how much dust i'll wipe off,
It doesn't matter how long it takes for you to get it.

As long as my heart is wrapped by your fingers,
As long as your ears hear my words,
As long as your eyes see my writing,
As long as your hands hold mine,

I don't care.

The worst part about saying hello to you, is never knowing when I'll say good-bye.

Hello.

Hear.

If words can cut deeper than a knife, then your tongue is a spoon.

Not a sharp syllable spoken from your tongue has an edge that leaves a mark.
Instead, it has the tenderness to carry vowels and consonants that heal and hug ears perfectly tight.

Your voice is like soup and crackers to an ill fallen child. It hugs and warms the ears and I'm oh so grateful to hear it every time.
Like a kid listening out for Santa's sleigh bells ringing I listen for any chance you might speak.

Every story you tell is my favorite because it's spoken with your voice and no story's end is bitter so long as you're ending it.
You make phones worth calling and sounds worth hearing, and if you could see noise then you'd make sights worth seeing.

But sights aren't too bad as it is I guess.
But that's only because when I see you, I might get to hear you too.

Peter Lopez

Blankets.

I'm glad we aren't talking.
I love you to death, and being friends with you is a bridge I'm glad we built but I'm glad
we aren't talking.

Your days are long, long enough to make the sun's journey across our sky seem
pointless when inside your mind it's raining day and night.
It's day and night and before you know it's night it's day once again and once again
you've gotten no rest.
But I'm glad we aren't talking.
I've got much to share and I love you to death so of course I chose you to share
but for once you're getting rest after a day where the sun was shining but winds were
blowing clouds where you stepped.

So I'm glad we aren't talking, because it means the clouds can't get you.
Your blankets will keep you dry.

Can't Help.

I can't wait to hear every sentence you say.
I can't wait to hear every story you tell.
I can't wait to hear you excited for the smallest reasons.
I can't wait to hear you call my name when you see me.
I can't wait to hear you in general because it will be something from you.

I can't help but notice the vibrant colors that make my heart beat just a little bit faster in the distant background of your eyes when in polaroid or person.

I can't help but stare and stare into the face that captured my heart and continue falling and falling in love.

I can't help but look at your hand in mine and think how is this real in a world so unforgiving that I know someone that makes it just a little more fair.

God, I can't help a lot of things.

Worthless.

If you were dirt,
You'd be the dirt that hides treasure.
if you were a raining cloud,
you'd be the cloud that makes flowers bloom the prettiest.
if you were a restless night,
you'd be a memorable sleep over.
If you were tears in eyes,
You'd be cry's from happiness.

Everything that's *you* just has a little more value to it.

Impossible.

Like singing in a tornado,
Like dancing on the clouds,
Like flirting with a fish,

Being away from you is impossible.

Rush.

I've always been a patient person.
I'm not in a rush to experience life.
And although I wonder what a kiss is like,
I'm in no hurry to have my first kiss.

I just never expected to want my first kiss to be you.

Things to say.

Maybe the day I stop caring is the day I'll stop writing.
Maybe that's why my pen moves.

Because when I run out of words to speak,
I'll still have things to say.

Peter Lopez

All the same.

You're nothing special.

You bleed blood.
You get sick.
You act needy.

I don't care.
I love you all the same.

Another Chance.

Every conversation could be our last.
We don't know when that will be;

So I'll love you like I'll never get another chance.

My love language is hearing your voice.
My love language is feeling your touch.
My love language is seeing the world through the reflection of your eyes.
My love language is tasting the food on our dates.
My love language is knowing the smells around me are yours.
My love language is enjoying the time you give me.
My love language is missing the time I couldn't take from you.
My love language is you.

It's everything about you.

Love Language.

Share.

The sun's warmth will mean nothing,
The wind's refreshing breeze will be pointless,
The flower's bloom won't have purpose,
The moon's beauty wouldn't be cared about, and
The holidays would run dry,

If I don't share those moments with you.

Peter Lopez

Greener.

The camera shines the brightest flashes when you're in frame.
The colors of a brush never run dry when painting you.
The sun gets mistaken for a moon when in pictures of you.

I don't know if you notice it,
But things are better if you're around.
That things of light are only shadows to what you make bright.

Or maybe it's my eyes out of focus until they find you.

Regardless, I'll always notice the grass is always greener wherever you step.

For You.

If your eyes made it rain,
I'd lay with the flowers and puddles.
If your smiles lit skies,
I'd fly with the planes and sing with the birds.
If your coughs made you a monster,
I'd dance in the dark and play under my bed.

Like a year passing you by, if you realize or not:
I'll be there for you no matter what.

Peter Lopez

Train.

You board my train of thought with no ticket.
You take your seat and you'll ride with no destination.
Sometimes you'll even drive the train elsewhere.
Most times I let you.

But every time you do,
I don't seem to mind.

Think.

My therapist helped me with my ADHD.
Kinda.

Apparently I'm severely ADHD, but my therapist helped me with it. I'm on some meds that are supposed to help me focus. They worked, and It's like all the several voices in my head talking to me just stopped.

Yours didn't.

You still linger around in the home you've built in my heart and occasionally visit my thoughts like you're grocery shopping.

I still can't focus; the only difference between them and now is that I can't think clearly anymore.
Because now the only thing I'm able to think clearly on is you.

You're so imperfect.

You have blemishes and a temper.

You're snappy and annoy me.

Like a thorn in my side or food in my teeth.

I love it.

The scars that perfect your body from an unforgiving life.

The drooping lines that strain your face that grow with age.

Your self doubt feeds your insecurities.

Its hunger blinds you to everything I see.

Where you see flaws and imperfections.

Blemishes that disgust you.

They may leave you disappointed.

I see nothing but beauty in a human.

Mark's unique to you that magnifies who you are and makes your skin your own.

It leaves me speechless and distraught.

How ever was I lucky to just see you as you are.

Just how perfectly imperfect, you're so flawlessly flawed.

Imperfect.

Yours.

What am I if not yours?

With a hand I desire to protect with my own.

To provide and to serve.

To love and to care.

To be yours

With lips I want to call mine.

With a love to share with my own.

With experiences to share and fingers to interlock.

What else is there if you are not mine?

Hearts Beat With Band-aids

I want all the silly things.

I want to remember your smile and picture it right before I sleep.

I want it to stay stuck in my mind like a photo shown off in a museum for so long it's started to collect dust.

I want to wake up and see your name as a notification on my phone.

I want it to be something stupid too.

Like you just text me asking "do you still love me?" as if I could ever stop.

Because then I could tell you…

I want all the silly things.

I could tell you that I want you to spam my phone when you're excited about something.

I could call you right then and there, and look you in the eyes over FaceTime and tell you that I want you to tell me all the costume ideas you have when it comes time for Halloween.

I could tell you right then and there, that if we do costumes, that we also have to wear pumpkin heads, and take stupid photos of us in our matching outfits.

That we could post that photo to every social media we have while next to each other, giggling like a kid trying to sleep right before Christmas Day.

I could tell you just how much I want these silly things.

It wouldn't stop there either.

We'd have to get matching pj's for winter, do small gift exchanges at a starbucks to celebrate Christmas.

We should have small arguments about what movies we're gonna watch, and in what order we do it while we snuggle under some blankets like to perfectly fit puzzle pieces.

So many silly, stupid, and even ironic and cringey things.

I want them all.

But more than that;

I want all the silly things,

To be done with you.

Silly things.

Hearts Beat With Band-aids

With me.

I'm scared

Scared to grow up

Scared to move out

Scared to get sick

Scared to change as a whole

I'm scared

Scared of the thought I'll do all these things.

The things I hate

The things I fear

The things I hesitate with

The things I'd do day to day

I'm just scared

But maybe if you're with me-

It won't be all that bad.

Alarm.

I get up and go about my day like every other boy.

I do everything I'd need or want to but when I see you.

I wonder if I did anything at all. I hear your laughter and your voice and I wait for my alarm. While I wait for this dream to end, I just stare, enjoying this unreal feeling in this unreal moment waiting for the walls to collapse upon themself as I open my eyes to the dark empty room and my alarm screaming.

But it never does, the alarm doesn't scream, and I don't shift my eyes from yours to my ceiling, and I never have to do it all over again.

Good thing I don't mind.

The days where the space in my eyes are not filled with the sights of you: will instead be filled with drops of rain, no matter how clear the skies may be.

After all, a day is dark if there's no sun: and all the plants will wilt.

Rain.

I love you.

I love you.

What a hard thing to say?

I don't hate you.

I don't resent you.

I adore everything about you.

I adore the way your eyes sparkle.

I adore the way your lips glow.

I adore the way your hair blooms.

And even the way it falls ever so perfectly.

Perfect.

That's what you are in the light of my eyes.

With nothing to resent but the time that is ever so fleeting when you're near.

So why is it so hard to say?

I love you.

I love you.

I love everything about you.

Hearts Beat With Band-aids

I don't want to die,

Just to drown in your arms.

I don't want to die,

Just for our fates to intertwine.

I just want a little bit more of your warmth.

Just a little bit more of your comfort.

Just a little bit more of the feeling when you're around.

Just a little bit more of you.

Want.

Would I pick you in a room full of girls?

God, if only it was just that.

In a bush brimming with berries,

I'd pick you over the sweetest of bundles.

For compared to your flavor,

Everything is bitter.

In a deck of the fanciest of cards,

And in a match against rules unfair

You are the only card I strive for,

And are the only ace I'd play.

If I must walk without you,

It would be towards your direction.

If I must stand alone,

It would be in excitement of your arrival.

Hearts Beat With Band-aids

If I couldn't walk to you,

I would crawl instead.

If I couldn't stand and wait for your presence to grace mine,

I'd sit in memory of the times you did.

I wouldn't just pick you in a room of girls,

I'd do it with a smile.

I'd do it with a smile,

Cause I know I picked the right one.

Pick.

To Whomever It Concerns

Love isn't always without consequences.
That's what makes it worth fighting for.

And should that fight be lost and a heart drop blood,

Time's a bandaid that's forever healing hearts that bleed.
It's a bandaid I'll never need to put on myself,
It's stuck to me and will stick with me regardless if I want it too.
It's on my heart regardless if you notice.

And it's okay, because hearts can beat with band-aids.

My heart will beat with band-aids,
And it will try and try to beat with the love it wants to give.
Then it falls off.

And with a band-aid off or even on you should love whomever needs it.
And while I love, I will write to whomever it concerns.

So to whomever it concerns, I promise you are worth every consequence I'll face,
every line I write, and every band-aid I might wear.

To whomever it concerns, I love you.

Author's Note.

Life isn't easy nor fair for anyone. You can learn that much at almost any age, and some learn it faster than others. I'm no special case, but I think together we can make living just a little more bearable and a little less unfair.

I'd be lying if I said I did it all on my own, I didn't. I had family and friends I could talk to, and if I couldn't talk to them, I found comfort from music made by *Boywithuke / Charley Yang* or content creators like streamers such as *Endo* and *Chumba* on twitch. Regardless of what it is for anyone who might be suffering or struggling, there is a place for you where you can belong. I think people suffer to give comfort to those who need it most and help them learn with a little less hurt. That's why I've decided to share my poetry.

Maybe I'm wrong and corny but if anything I've learned to be okay with myself and that means anyone can too. Or maybe I'm just another foolish poet.

www.ingramcontent.com/pod-product-compliance
Lightning Source LLC
Chambersburg PA
CBHW051058250726
48656CB00001B/354